ME AND MY POEMS

For Sophie & Chloe
Enjoy this book, or your
mum will have wasted her
money on you... AGAIN!

ME AND MY POEMS

58 poems

by

Nick Toczek

ISBN-13: 978-0-9559711-0-5

Typeset in Chaparral by Decent Typesetting Ltd,
Lime Kiln Business Centre, High Street,Wootton Bassett SN4 7HF

Printed in the UK by CPI Bookmarque, Croydon, CR0 4TD

The paper and board used in the paperback by Caboodle Books Ltd are natural recyclable products made from wood grown in sustainable forests. The manufacturing processes conform to the environmental regulations of the country of origin.

Caboodle Books Ltd
Riversdale, 8 Rivock Avenue, Steeton, BD20 6SA
TEL 01535 656015

Contents

Self-Portrait

I'm a bearded, bald asthmatic.
I've an office in my attic.
I'm a poet and magician,
Swim to stay in good condition.

I'm writing an opera for The Proms.
When people ask where Toczek's from
I look at them as if they're mad
Then say: "I got it from my dad!"

I'm a stand-up comic. I play pool.
I think hot curries are really cool.
I present a weekly music show
(Though just on local radio).

I'm Grandpa Nick. I'm vegetarian,
Got more books than a librarian
Yet I'm a slow and restless reader.
Oh... and I used to be a dragon-breeder*.

---

*TRUE! I bred bearded dragons (Australian lizards)
and sold them to pet shops.

Nobody Here

Where's Jed? Still in bed.
Where's John? Come and gone.
Where's Jean? Not been seen.
Where's Jan? In Japan.
Where's Joan? On the phone.
Where's Jack? Won't be back.

Where's Jake? On his break.
Where's Jill? Absent still.
Where's Jude? Fetching food.
Where's Joy? Out with Roy.
Where's Jim? Cops took him.
Where's Jay? Went away.

Where's James? Playing games.
Where's Jess? Changed address.
Where's Jock? Died of shock.
Where's Jane? Can't explain.
Where's Jules? Broke the rules.
Where's Jill? Absent still.

Where's Jade? Been delayed.
Where's June? Honeymoon.
Where's Jen? Gone again.
Where's Judd? Caked in mud.
Where's Jem? Bethlehem.
Where's Josh? Somewhere posh.

Where's Joe? Had to go.
Where's Jeff? Oh-eff-eff.
Where's Jazz? Meeting Baz.
Where's Joss? With the boss.
Where's Jez? Sick, he says.
Where's Jeb? On The Web.

Where are you? On the loo.

Dinah And The Dinosaur

When Dinah saw a dinosaur
She told her mum who paused before
She firmly locked the patio door
And hid the china in a drawer
Cos strangers make her insecure.

When Dinah saw a dinosaur
She told her dad who scratched his jaw
And asked what kind of clothes it wore
Then, glancing down the corridor,
Said: "That's enough. We'll say no more."

When Dinah saw a dinosaur
She told her gandpapa who swore
And slapped his thigh and roared: "Heehaw!"
And danced around the kitchen floor
Till grandma called him immature.

When Dinah saw a dinosaur
She told her great-aunt Eleanor
Who telephoned her son-in-law
Who said: "They're French, so try 'bonjour'."
He'd lived in France before the war.

Now Dinah wasn't actually sure
Exactly what it was she saw
And, anyhow, you can't set store
By what she sees. Her eyesight's poor.
She's been wrong several times before.

And the dinosaur that Dinah saw,
Which might have been a herbivore,
A passing bus, a Labrador
Or something else we could ignore,
Crushed a building with its claw.

Street Poem

I'm a street
a high street
and my pavements are concrete.
I'm complete
-ly straight
no bends,
and I've junctions at both ends.

At my lights,
red, green
and amber,
people cross
my two-inch
camber.
I give them
the right
of way
to get from Boots
to C
and A.

Between twelve
and three,
you can't park
on me,
except to load
or else
unload.

You can hit
the road
but you sure can't beat this street.
I'm police
controlled,
meter-maid
patrolled,
local coun
-cil kept,
maintained,
fully-drained
and swept.

Ghost Town

From the back-streets down by the aqueduct
Come the undead ones with their blood all sucked.
They've a dreadful smell. They don't look well.
Their souls are sold to him from Hell.
They've grown stone-cold and their eyes are glazed.
When they sense warm flesh, they become half-crazed.
They're just like something from a horror movie.
If they weren't so real, they'd be really groovy.

They're dead but they won't lie down.
They're dead but they won't lie down.
They're in our town and they're walking round.
They're dead but they won't lie down.

Wherever we go, they're in hot pursuit,
So we stab, we shoot, we electrocute,
To no avail, though. God knows why,
They refuse point-blank to properly die.
We can't even go to the supermarket.
They crowd round the car when we try to park it.
The dog got out and can't be found
Though we can hear it howling underground.

They're dead but they won't lie down.
They're dead but they won't lie down.
They're in our town and they're walking round.
They're dead but they won't lie down.

Their clothes are lousy, their complexions vile.
They're the walking weird. They've got no style.
They're out all night with their clanking chains.
They eat eyeballs whole and they suck out brains.
And we can't now phone cos they've cut the wires.
And they've crashed the car and slashed the tyres.
And we can't relax cos of all their screams.
When we finally sleep, they invade our dreams.

They're dead but they won't lie down.
They're dead but they won't lie down.
They're in our town and they're walking round.
They're dead but they won't lie down.

There's a demon in the attic. In the cellar there's
    a ghoul.
And there's something in the bathroom that's
    decidedly uncool.
And *you* don't look too good. Are those maggots in
    your hair?
And I'm staring in the mirror, but my reflection
    isn't there.

We're dead but we won't lie down.
We're dead but we won't lie down.
We're in your town and we're walking round.
We're dead but we won't lie down.

Poem To Read While You Wait

Wait at the bus stop.
Wait in the rain.
Wait on the journey to
Wait for the train.
Wait while it takes you to
Wait for your plane.
Wait at the flight gate.
Wait there in vain.
Wait and wait and wait and wait
And wait and wait again.

Wait at the help desk.
Wait to complain.
Wait while the staff there
Wait to explain.
Wait with your passport.
Wait but remain.
Wait till the waiting
Drives you insane.
Wait and wait and wait and wait
And wait and wait again.

Wait on the tarmac.
Wait on the plane.
Wait while the plane's weight
Takes the flight lane.
Wait for a cloud-break.
Wait to see terrain.
Wait while you circle.
Wait to land again.
Wait and wait and wait and wait
And wait and wait again.

Wait in the gangway
Wait to leave the plane.
Wait for your suitcase.
Waiting is a pain.
Wait with a headache.
Wait while your brain
Waits to see if waiting
Triggers your migraine.
Wait and wait and wait and wait
And wait and wait again.

Yeah And Boo

(after *Things To Cheer And Boo* by John Coldwell)

I've got you a Playstation...	Yeah!
But there's a power cut.	Boo!
So I've bought you a Nintendo Wii...	Yeah!
But there's still a power cut.	Boo!
The power cut's finished...	Yeah!
But the Nintendo Wii's broken.	Boo!
You can use the Playstation instead...	Yeah!
Oh no you can't, your dad's on it.	Boo!
I've got some chewing gum for you...	Yeah!
Cos I've finished with it *(offering it from my mouth)*	Boo!
I've brought you home a pizza...	Yeah!
I found it in the bin at the back of Pizza Hut.	Boo!
You can play out with your friends	Yeah!
Only joking.	Boo!
Okay, you can play out with your friends...	Yeah!
For half a minute.	Boo!
You can watch whatever you like on TV...	Yeah!
So long as it's the news.	Boo!
And you can stay up late tonight...	Yeah!
To tidy your room.	Boo!

Advice For Spacemen

When you test your rocket
Oil the engine sprocket*
They can't replace
In outer space,
Shops up there don't stock it.

When you fly your rocket
Time your flight and clock it.
Don't exceed
Hyper-speed.
Safety first. Don't mock it.

When you park your rocket
Do watch where you dock it.
The Spaceway Code
Says: off the road,
Otherwise, you block it.

When you mend your rocket
Don't hammer it or knock it.
Just read the rules
On robot tools
Then plug them in the socket.

When you leave your rocket
Don't forget to lock it.
The only place
For keys in space
Is in your trouser pocket.

* Sprockets are the teeth on a gear-wheel,
like the ones that slot into a bicycle-chain.

Cars In Cairo

While mid-day sun's
bright blazing heat
makes ovens of
each fume-filled street,
out we go in
cars in Cairo.
Windows down we
still perspire. Oh,
feel as if we've
all caught fire. Oh,
save us – please – from
cars in Cairo.

Jammed in, rammed in,
bumped and bashed in,
crammed in, crushed in,
crashed and smashed in,
grind of gear and
skid of tyre. Oh,
no escaping
cars in Cairo.

Zig-zag swerving,
quite unnerving,
honking, horning,
loudly serving
every warning
ever since first
thing this morning,
hooting like a
crazy choir. Oh,
there's no muting
cars in Cairo.

Tourist coaches:
More mad driving.
Parties leaving
or arriving
run the risk of
not surviving.
Horse-drawn loads
and hand-carts heaving,
scooters, bikes and
walkers weaving
wildly like a
writer's biro
through the queues of
cars in Cairo.

Mini-buses,
yellow cabs and
limos owned by
rich Arabs and
sweating cops with
whistles blowing
try to keep this
traffic flowing,
coming, going,
speeding, slowing,
to-ing, fro-ing
cars in Cairo,
those we own and
those we hire. Oh,
far too many
cars in Cairo.

We're not cursed by
Tutankhamen.
Here we're cursed by
tooting car men,
deafened by the
din so dire. Oh,
bellowed by the
cars in Cairo.

When I Was A Pirate

And when I was a pirate
One of my legs was wooden.
Since then it's grown back again
Though doctors said it couldn't.

And when I was a pirate
I'd a parrot that could talk,
But now I'm dad to seven kids
Who only screech and squawk.

And when I was a pirate
I sailed the seven seas,
But now I wait at bus stops
And shop at Sainsbury's.

And when I was a pirate
I wore a black eye-patch,
But now I need my glasses on
To watch a football match.

And when I was a pirate
I was scary with a sword.
Now I go: "Excuse me please!"
But only get ignored.

And when I was a pirate
I owned a treasure chest,
But now I earn a weekly wage
And bank it with NatWest.

And when I was a pirate
My coat was spun from gold,
But now I wear an anorak
With the hood up when it's cold.

And when I was a pirate
I was hairy, with a beard,
But now my head is shiny
And my hair has disappeared.

And when I was a pirate
I had one hand and a hook,
But, the day that we were married,
That's the first thing my wife took.
She said: "Get real! You'll need both hands
To wash and clean and cook!"

And when I was a pirate
I was merciless and cruel...
And I still am, because I make
My children go to school!

Crusher

I'm a
huge hy-
draulic
crusher.

Read my
base I'm
made in
Russia.

Oiled out
of a
Texas
gusher.

Piston
puller.
Piston
pusher.

Function
like a
toilet
flusher.

I'm a
huge hy-
draulic
crusher.

Made to
be a
metal
musher.

My sur-
roundings
could be
plusher.

Scrap-yard
mud that
should be
lusher.

I work
slowly
I'm no
rusher.

I'm a
huge hy-
draulic
crusher.

Travel Sickness

Sick in the taxi
Sick on the train
Sick in the airport
Sick on the plane
Sick on the coach
And sick again.

Sick six times
From here to Spain.

The End Of School

We shove gloves and scarves on.
It's shivery and stark.
And out in the playground
It's evening and dark.
We rattle the railings
With sticks for a lark.

The sky's grown as gray
As the skin of a shark.
The branches are bare
On the trees in the park.
The wind took their leaves
Leaving winter-proof bark.

The streetlights are waking
And making their mark.
At first they're a dull red
And glow like a spark,
Grow orange, then yellow –
A dazzling arc.

"They're forecasting snow",
I heard one mum remark.
Sleet comes, then the bus comes.
We loudly embark.
The sunshine of summer's
Fled south like the lark.

Invisible Riddle

What's got one eye
In the middle of its nose
And you can hear it
But you can't see it?

Answer: noise

Outdoor Riddle

Who were the soldiers
Tall and erect
Who came to your door
While you still slept?
Who were they
So pale and thin
Who never knocked
To be let in,
But stood on guard
In hats of tin?

Answer: milkbottles

All Right

Start on the right foot. "Righty-oh!" you said.
A bit-of-alright, and by the right, but not right in the head.

Left, right! Birth-right. Right-hand man.
Marry the man who's Mr. Right, if you can.

Can't put a foot right. Get right along.
Right of entry. Right you are! Whether we're right or wrong.

See you right. Serves you right. In your right mind.
On the right side of him. It's right, I think you'll find.

Step in the right direction. Am I right as rain?
Are you right as ninepence? Right you are, again!

We're downright upright. Go right into town.
Give your right arm for this and write it down.

Shopping List

Ox tongue, ox tail
And Wensleydale
And curly kale
And ginger ale

And jugs of jam
And legs of ham
And slabs of lamb
And kegs of Spam

Gaggles of greens
And bags of beans
And tons of tins
Of tangerines

Coffees and teas
Toffees and peas
And choose more cheese
Cheddars and bries

And ladle spoons
Of macaroons
And crates of dates
And plates of prunes

And lollypops
And lemon drops
And salad crops
And turnip tops

And bread to fry
And fruit to dry
Mustard powder
Custard powder

Chocolate éclairs
And nuts and pears
Honey from bees
And soft lychees

And crispy toast
And nuts to roast
And ready meals
And jellied eels

And much more meat
And shredded wheat
And some small treat
That's sweet to eat

Pickles and pies
And mince and fries
Some chicken legs
Some quince, some eggs

A ripened lime
Some tripe, some thyme
And fudge and salmon
And figs and gammon

And hurry home. I'm hungry.

The Yeti's Verse

Dante Gabriel Rossetti
Wrote that once his great-aunt Betty

Met a vet who'd met a Yeti
Somewhere on the Serengeti.

On a jetty sat this Yeti,
Large and listless, fat and fretty,

Wrapped in hair like thick spaghetti,
Dropping dandruff like confetti.

Sunlight made the Yeti sweaty,
Argumentative and petty.

Yet when day became sunsetty,
He wrote poems and libretti.

And, all night, you'd hear the Yeti
Typing on an Olivetti.

History Of Love

When we first met, I couldn't talk
Because I was Neanderthal
Voicing love through grunt and squawk
You couldn't understand at all.

But even though you didn't reply,
I thought our love would never die.

Later, I was Neolithic,
Finding rocks on which I drew
Pictures saying you're terrific
And I sent them all to you.

But even though you didn't reply,
I thought our love would never die.

Loving you in ancient Egypt
From The Temple of Osiris,
I sent you hieroglyphic script
That I'd scribbled on papyrus.

But even though you didn't reply,
I thought our love would never die.

And then, throughout the siege of Troy,
I wrote you, every day,
Mycenaean symbols of love's joy
On tablets baked in clay.

But even though you didn't reply,
I thought our love would never die.

I served in Roman legions
On remote empire patrols
And, from these hostile regions,
I sent you Latin scrolls.

But even though you didn't reply,
I thought our love would never die.

Writing, at length, from a longboat
As a Viking with a liking for Norse,
Our love was the story I wrote
And I sent you that saga, of course.

But even though you didn't reply,
I thought our love would never die.

In 1066, as a Norman,
A Frenchman who'd conquered the Brits,
I sewed tapestries brightly informing
The world that I loved you to bits.

But even though you didn't reply,
I thought our love would never die.

On a pilgrimage to Canterbury
I mailed you a hand-written card,
It read: "My dear, please answer me.
This loving in silence is hard."

But even though you didn't reply,
I thought our love would never die.

Last night I called and left a message
On your Ansaphone
To say I'm going out and doubt
That I will dance alone.

But even though you didn't reply,
I thought our love would never die.

Today, while on The Internet,
I sent you an e-mail
To say goodbye because I've met
A *talkative* female.

I am a prose poem.
This is my second line,
And this my third.

I consist of fifteen lines in all,
These made up from a total
Of seventy one words.

I am neither beautiful
Nor am I ugly
And I differ from all other poems
In that I describe nothing
Except myself.

Where when and by whom I was written
Is therefore unimportant.

I have no title, and finish
Abruptly.

The Boom-Boom-Boom
From Susan's Room
which finally grew too loud to bear

When parents cup their ears and frown
And scream: "Child! Turn your music down!"
Most shout in vain. Their words just drown
While house-walls tremble all round town
And chimneys sway and lampposts shake
And those who'd sleep are kept awake
Mistaking it for an earthquake
As pictures fall and mirrors break
And flowers wilt which were in bloom
And doom and gloom appear to loom
And all because twin speakers boom
From in a teenager's bedroom.

But there was once one case much worse,
A din so dangerous and perverse
That no exploding universe
Nor any Hellish devil's curse
Could ever hope to sound as bad.
The rock that roared from Susan's pad
Left neighbours dead or deaf or mad.
There's never been a room that's had
So many speakers stuffed in it
And while they blared, she'd sit and hit
Like in an epileptic fit
The loudest bits of her drum-kit.

"Our Susan's odd," her parents said
"Because she once fell out of bed
And hit her head and bled and bled
And turned her bedroom carpet red.
Since then she's never played with toys
And isn't interested in boys.
In fact, there's nothing she enjoys
Apart from making loads of noise.
We say: "Find friends." She never heeds.
She won't watch TV, seldom reads.
Loudspeakers now are all she needs
And drums and loads of speaker-leads."

One day, by way of booster packs,
She raised the row to a new max
And played one of her loudest tracks
And, as it reached its mad climax,
Roof-slates tumbled, windows smashed,
Whole house-bricks crumbled, mortar mashed.
Her parents fled, both bruised and gashed,
And then the entire building crashed...
But once that weight had downward rushed
The neighbourhood seemed strangely shushed
Because, beneath, poor Sue lay crushed,
Her and her music wholly hushed.

Be warned, then, if you're in your teens.
Play your rock music by all means,
But speakers packed in like sardines
Will smash you into smithereens.

Living In A Tower Block

Elevator power,
It's elevator power.
This is what we need
When we're living in a tower.

Elevator power,
Yes, elevator power
Has lifts in motion
Every minute of the hour.

Elevator power,
It's elevator power
That carries our cleaners
To where they scrub and scour.

Elevator power,
Yes, elevator power,
Suitable for anyone
With floors to devour.

Elevator power,
It's elevator power
That carries people down
Like droplets in a shower.

Elevator power,
Yes, elevator power
That pushes people skyward
Like a growing flower.

Elevator power,
It's elevator power
Delivering our pizzas
And our sweet'n'sour.

Elevator power,
Yes, elevator power
This is what we need
When we're living in a tower.

The Total Flop

(for high-jumper Dick Fosbury whose famous
'Fosbury Flop' won him Olympic gold in 1968)

In sport I'm for the high-jump,
No Fosbury, just a flop.
Got dropped from the karate team.
They've given me the chop.

I go-karted so slowly
That the engine simply rusted.
I tried to throw the discus,
Was so bad I got disgusted.

I'm useless on the tennis court
I just can't stand the racket.
I've had it with computer sport,
Given up, can't hack it.

I hurt my neck while batting,
Should've known I'd crick it.
And football's my addiction,
But I wish that I could kick it.

I used to play some snooker
But my game has gone to pot.
Yachting wasn't right for me –
I felt an idi-yacht.

I had a go at fencing
But merely caused a fence.
Tried to lift a hundred pounds
But only raised ten pence.

Hold on though, I think at last
My bad luck's going to stop.
They're hanging out their rugby shirts
And want me for a prop!

Why Plants Can't Move

In days before the world was treed,
When birch and beech were less than seed,
The tallest plants were fern and reed.

A fight broke out, unrefereed,
Between a flower and a weed –
The two, it seemed, had disagreed.

They slapped and kicked and punched and kneed
Which terrified the centipede
And caused a mini-beast stampede.

Then God got very cross indeed.
And thunder crashed as he decreed
Strong roots for flower and for weed.

He took their legs, denied them speed,
Cos that way peace was guaranteed.
That's why the flower and the weed

Stare heavenwards. They pray, they plead
To be forgiven and be freed,
But God pays neither any heed.

Frog Snoggers

Fair fairy-tale princesses
Were forever kissing frogs,
Were blind to uglinesses,
To complexions like wart-hogs,
Got dirt all down their dresses
From frog-frolicking in bogs.

How could they kiss those slavering lips
That guzzled flies from foul tongue-tips?
How could they form relationships with frogs?

Fair fairy-tale princesses,
Out in rainstorms and thick fogs,
Seemed hardly royal highnesses
In their wet and filthy togs.
As amphibians' mistresses,
They were treated worse than dogs.

With all that spit that slopped in drips
From fat and flabby floppy lips,
How could they form relationships with frogs?

Fair fairy-tale princesses,
With much muck upon their clogs,
Had pond-weeds, water-cresses
And green slimes from stones and logs
All tangled in their tresses
From pursuing froggy snogs.

Enduring slushy stagnant dips
In search of croaking belching lips,
How could they form relationships with frogs?

Tom's Thumb

which was attached to his body

Tom, because he sucked his thumb
Day and night, upset his mum.
Left no space to let food in,
Plug-in-mouth, he grew too thin.

Couldn't swallow, couldn't chew.
What could his poor mother do?
Nothing! Not a single crumb
Found its way into his tum.

But then hunger bit young Tom.
Where would his next meal come from?
He'd got just one thing to eat,
In his mouth, one piece of meat.

Seconds later, there's Tom's thumb
Sucked right down into his tum
With four fingers and one palm
Followed by their wrist and arm,

Shoulders, other arm and chest
And, before he could protest,
Waist and hips and legs and feet.
What next for his lips to eat?

Not a pudding, but instead
The last of Tom... Yes, his head,
Leaving nothing of the lad.
So, be warned, thumb-sucking's bad!

Indoor Riddle

His hands on his face, his back to the wall,
Your father's father's dark and tall.
So who is he? It's time to tell...
And he's the one who tells it well.

Answer: a grandfather clock

Sliding On The Ice

When weather's at it's winterest
The game to grab our interest
That's zoomiest and sprinterest
To keep us warm and feeling nice
Is sliding on the ice.
I've said it once,
I'll say it twice:
We're sliding on the ice.

So when the air is nippiest,
The frozen ground the slippiest
And tumbliest and trippiest,
Then our idea of paradise
Is sliding on the ice.
I've said it once,
I'll say it twice:
We're sliding on the ice.

Yes, when our breath is cloudiest,
You'll find us at our rowdiest,
Our loudiest and crowdiest.
The explanation, in a trice,
Is sliding on the ice.
I've said it once,
I'll say it twice:
We're sliding on the ice.

The Visitor

Whenever the reader says: "What is it...?",
the listeners shout: "It's an alien!"

It's people-shaped, a scaly 'un,
A grey and sort of snaily 'un.

What is it...? **It's an alien!**

A slightly slimy-traily 'un
That's clearly not mammalian.

What is it...? **It's an alien!**

A far from everydaily 'un,
It's more a fairytaly 'un.

What is it...? **It's an alien!**

Its voice is quite a waily 'un,
A sing-song nightingaly 'un.

What is it...? **It's an alien!**

It doesn't sound Australian
Or Finnish or Westphalian.

What is it...? **It's an alien!**

No Arab or Israeli 'un
Or cheesy Wensleydaly 'un.

What is it...? **It's an alien!**

What is it...? **It's an alien!**

What is it...? **It's an alien!**

Keep In Touch

You come to call
But don't at all
There's no one at the door
And I'm away
Till yesterday
But could be back before.

Don't write because
Where I just was
I won't be any more
So letters sent
To where I went
I won't know who they're for.

I'll phone last week
When we won't speak
Except in words galore
That, though unsaid
Or heard or read,
None of us can ignore.

The Big Parade

In the big parade there were
Seventy-six trombones and xylophones,
Seventy-six children with ice-cream cones,
Seventy-six Aunt Janes and Jeans and Joans,
Seventy-six men using mobile phones,
Seventy-six Lion Kings on Lion King thrones,
Seventy-six pop stars with microphones,
Seventy-six pale ghosts and their tombstones,
Seventy-six Playstation levels and zones,
Seventy-six punk bands called The Undertones,
Seventy-six pirate ships flying skull 'n' crossbones
Seventy-six Harry Potters with philosophers' stones,
And seventy-six young children giving loud groans,
Packed off to bed with moody moans.

Ecology Rant

Ecology rant. Ecology rave.
This isn't a joke. It's really grave.
Go energy save, go energy save.

This planet's our home. It isn't our slave.
We'll change our style, be bold, be brave
And energy save, and energy save.

I'll use less water when I shave
Or when I brush my teeth and bathe.
I'll energy save, I'll energy save.

I'll share my car with Sue and Dave.
And close that door! This isn't a cave!
Let's energy save, let's energy save.

There's power in fire and wind and wave
To give us the things we really crave
And, in return, we'll energy save.

We'll cut our waste from birth to grave.
It's how the whole world should behave
And energy save, and energy save.

Ecology rant. Ecology rave.
Let's energy, energy, energy save.

Riddle: Who Am I?

I've always been extremely thin
Yet I contain the room I'm in
Though it's untouched by hand or din.

And I have got the smoothest skin.
It's shiny, like a fish's fin.
To look at, I could be your twin.

To find the word that's me just spin
Six letters, but you must begin
By making sure I've three R's in.

Answer: a mirror

The Truth About Giants

They've found the full fossil
Of someone colossal
Or so the newspapers inform us –

A heap of huge stones
They claim were the bones
Of somebody simply ginormous

Perhaps it was Glenda Stupendous
Whose temper, they say, was horrendous;

Or Gemma Gigantic
Who drank The Atlantic;

Or Riminy-Diminy-Blimmin-Immense
Who talked and talked but made no sense;

Or Max and Meg, the Mountain Twins,
Who wore tyrannosaurus skins;

Or Tony Untiny Titanic,
So manic he'd make mammoths panic;

Or (ever-so-elegant and divine)
The Lady Eleanor Elephantine;

Or baritone Vincent Valentine Vast,
The blast of whose voice was unsurpassed;

Or else the bulk of Harry The Hulk,
A rogue of an ogre who'd lurk and skulk;

Or grumpy Grandma Grandiose –
Verbose and moody, rude and gross;

Or maybe Mister Biggerty-Big
Who wore a forest for a wig;

Or Agatha Tabitha Titan
Whose bottom was bigger than Brighton;

Or maybe Bob and Brenda Whopping
With twenty tons of weekly shopping;

Or Angus Bibangus Bubungus Humungus
Whose fifty-foot feet were fluffy with fungus

Or somebody else incredibly tall.
The thing about giants is none of them's small.

And every word of this is true
Or I'm not a toothbrush, and neither are you.

Puddle

The moon, the stars, the clouds, a plane
And all that my sky can contain
Reflected in a pool of rain.

This is the eye that follows the sky.

A sheet lain on the bare terrain
That's picture-smooth and mirror-plain
Like looking through a window-pane.

This is the mouth that swallows the sky.

Brilliant echo, bright refrain
Each tiny detail you retain
Write it down and tell it again.

This is the hand that borrows the sky.

Reflected in a pool of rain
My sky with what it can contain:
A bird, the sun, a plane again.

On A Flying Visit To Jakarta

My journey to Java's
Seen me fly so far to
Stay here for a few days
In central Jakarta.

I set off on foot to
Locate a bazaar to
Buy myself some bargains
And shop in a mart, I

Now stand at the crossroads.
This is a non-starter.
No local would wait here.
They're quicker. They're smarter.

They move like a rocket
If they ever are to
Get through all the traffic
That clogs up Jakarta.

This dangerous business
Could make me a martyr,
But I'll be a weaver,
A dodger, a darter

Who learns how to slip
Between bike, bus and car to
Get round town on two feet
While here in Jakarta.

When caught in the heat in
The heart of Jakarta,
I drink a whole carton
Of juice of tomato,

But won't pay the full price,
The art is to barter.
That's all part of life on
The streets of Jakarta.

Though I've been to Cairo,
Seen Naples and Sparta;
It's better by far to
Be here in Jakarta.

Soon, sadly, I'll pack and
Prepare for departure,
Then head for the airport
And fly from Jakarta.

Moody Mrs Moanypants

Moody Mrs Moanypants
From Sudbury in Surrey
Makes a meal of many things.
That woman loves to worry.

Moody Mrs Moanypants
Forever in a flurry,
Married Murray Moanypants
But soon had him to bury.

Moody Mrs Moanypants,
Who hates the taste of curry,
Cancels paying council tax
Because they're dumping slurry.

Moody Mrs Moanypants
All scamper, scuttle, scurry,
Says: "You're in my way, so move!"
Because she's in a hurry.

Moody Mrs Moanypants
From Sudbury in Surrey
Makes a meal of many things.
That woman loves to worry.

Watching Merlin

Watch the world-famous wizard called Merlin.
Note the way his white whiskers are curling.
See the star-spangled cloak he's unfurling.
Spot the rubies and mother-of-pearl in
That mysterious wand which he's twirling.

Stand witness to the wizard called Merlin
Catch the mad mist around him that's curling,
How his casting of spells sets it swirling,
But beware when it really starts whirling.
Fear the force of the curses he's hurling.

Winter Walking

When we walk out in winter weather
Across the moors, the gorse, the heather
We ride no horse, untie no tether
When we walk out in winter weather.

When we walk out in winter weather
We ride no horse, untie no tether
We're wearing neither fur nor feather
When we walk out in winter weather.

When we walk out in winter weather
We're wearing neither fur nor feather
We wrap in wool, with boots of leather
When we walk out in winter weather.

When we walk out in winter weather
We wrap in wool, with boots of leather
To keep well warm, we cling together
When we walk out in winter weather.

When we walk out in winter weather
To keep well warm, we cling together
Across the moors, the gorse, the heather
When we walk out in winter weather.

Grandma's Strange Machine

An advert in a magazine
Appealed to Grandma Geraldine.
We had our doubts, but she was keen
And sent off for her strange machine.

The parts were sent from Aberdeen.
They came wrapped up in polythene
To keep them dry, rust-free and clean.
We counted them. There were umpteen.

"Quite right!" said Grandma Geraldine,
Moving an antique figurine.
"Now bring my tool-kit here, Kathleen,
And take those chairs through there, Eugene."

Then, putting on her gabardine,
She spread a sheet of crinoline
Where all her furniture had been
And started building her machine.

Twelve hours passed... perhaps thirteen
When: "Nearly done!" said Geraldine,
Screwing a grommet in between
Two sprockets on the mezzanine.

Her room now seemed a submarine
That hummed like some smooth limousine
And glowed an eerie kind of green
Which came from a computer screen.

She oiled the joints with margarine
And filled both tanks with gasoline
Then stood well back, surveyed the scene,
And said: "I love its shiny sheen."

We cried: "But, Grandma Geraldine.
What do those words and numbers mean
That keep appearing on that screen?
And why've you built this strange machine?"

She paused while wiping her hands clean,
Said: "Children, please don't intervene!"
Then, climbing into her machine,
She sent us home... "Where have you been?"

Our parents asked. "At Geraldine's,"
We said, explaining what we'd seen
And all about her strange machine,
Its sounds, its smells, its bright green screen.

Well, years have passed. I'm now nineteen.
Flats were built where her house had been.
It disappeared. We've not since seen
Or heard one word from Geraldine.

Six Alphabet Riddles

1. What begins with a bee and ends with a wise head?

2. What does the alphabet become in a desert?

3. What fruit and veg can you find in an alphabet?

4. Where does the C meet the D?

5. What has a lot of Ns and Us as well as pairs of Gs?

6. What do you and I have between us?

Answers:

1. The alphabet (begins with AB and ends with YZ).

2. ABCDEFGPQRSTUVWXYZ (with no H to O).

3. Lettuce, a pea and a lemon (letters: a P and LMN).

4. South of The Wirral (where The River Dee flows into The Irish Sea).

5. A farm (hens and ewes and geegees).

6. JKLMNOPQRST (between I and U).

It's Festival Time

A festival! A festival!
A friendly, family festival.
The time of year that's best of all.

A festival! A festival!
Forget all things detestable
And dance in clothes majestical.
Your worries are divestistible.

A festival! A festival!
A friendly, family festival.
The time of year that's best of all.

A festival! A festival!
When food is most digestible,
And games are all contestable,
And presents are requestable.

A festival! A festival!
A friendly, family festival.
The time of year that's best of all.

A festival! A festival!
Sing songs and sound celestial.
Religions east and west have all
Got days they call a festival.

A festival! A festival!
A friendly, family festival.
The time of year that's best of all.
A festival!   A festival!

The Day That Nature
Took Things Back

On the day that nature took things back
My mum almost had a heart attack.
She woke with worms in her silk nightdress
And the whole of her bed in a total mess.
It was more like a farm or a forest or a park
Cos while she'd slept, under cover of dark,
Her headboard sprouted twigs and bark.
There were clumps of plants in the cotton sheeting,
Then the blanket budged and started bleating
And the eiderdown began to quack
On the day that nature took things back.

Downstairs, the rooms she'd carefully styled
Were unrecognizable and wild.
Our dog had become a wolf. It howled.
Our cat, grown large, had a mane. It growled.
Each slunk from room to room. They prowled.
So the parrot quickly quit its perch
And left the house and went in search
Of a mate in the greenhouse which, being warmed,
Was a jungle now where insects swarmed.
We had to hack ourselves a track
On the day that nature took things back.

Outside was like some place unknown.
The roads were wrecked and overgrown.
The street-lamps were all hung with vines,
The telegraph poles were now tall pines,
And birds were nesting on the traffic signs.
And every car and bus and truck
Was now no more than a heap of muck,
Each part gone back to what it was before
Meaning mostly oil and iron ore.
And every street in every town
Was similarly tumbledown,
From motorway to cul-de-sac,
On the day that nature took things back.

The grocer's shop produced confusion:
Fruit and veg grew in profusion,
While from the butcher's came all sorts
Of moos and grunts and oinks and snorts.
But none pulled pints and none bought shorts
On the corner in The Horse And Hounds
Where no one served or ordered rounds
As bottles burst or lost their caps
And branches thrust from barrel-taps
And crates of cans lost ring-pull tops
As apples, barley, grapes and hops
Hatched, high as harvest, from them all.
And, where it hung on the bar-room wall,
The stag's head gave a mating call
Denying death by the huntsman's pack
On the day that nature took things back.

The Chinese restaurant down our street
Had bamboo shooting several feet
Above its roof and chimney-tops
While the ground floor sprouted Eastern crops
Unlike those in adjoining shops.
There were chestnuts, mushrooms, beans and rice,
And herbs and spices that smelt nice.
And, now no longer sliced or diced,
But restored by nature's new device
Pigs and cattle roamed pagoda'd lawns
While Peking ducks on the lake caught prawns
Then a shark's fin surfaced, like in Jaws,
And I wished that I was safe indoors
As the whole of reality began to crack
On the day that nature took things back.

The Usual Place
(a truthful poem)

I'm reading and writing
Where no one can foil it,
Where no interruption
Can butt in and spoil it,
A place that is flutter-free,
Nutter-free, clutter-free.

My concentration
Needs silence to oil it,
So I've locked the door.
I'm enthroned on the toilet
A place that is chatter-free,
Natter-free, clatter-free.

Reading and writing
Where no-one can spoil it.
Reading and writing
While sat on the toilet.

A Dragon Describes Itself

This bag my body's bundled in
It isn't made of simple skin
But scale and ridge and rut and fin
As if of some twin origin
Like cockroach crossed with terrapin
Or coelacanth with sea urchin
Or armadillo and gherkin
Entwined by magic medicine.

This bag my body's bundled in
It isn't made of simple skin.
When winter famine leaves me thin -
A sad and sorry specimen -
It wrinkles round my shank and shin
Like thickened sheets of tarpaulin,
All pallid and tuberculin
As if I've been on heroin.

This bag my body's bundled in
It isn't made of simple skin
But hangs in folds below my chin
Which tighten when I roar or grin.
My smile, though, isn't genuine,
It comes from deep and dark within
From where my breath – part paraffin –
Explodes like nitroglycerine.

Romantic Poem

"When you try relationships,
What's it like to kiss their lips?

Is it true that your heart skips?
Do sun and moon and stars eclipse?"

"No, they taste of fish and chips!"

Roomers

"A view herd thin ewes?"

"There shore summit zap end."

"Wear zit go win gone?"

"Watt sit taller bout?"

"Wide know once top pit?"

"Scan Dallas. Their snow a there whirred four writ."

"Eye mutter lid is custard."

"Meat who, an dime knot a loan."

"Know yawn otter low gnat tall. Act Julie Al otter fuss arc um plea telly discus Ted whither low dove these Tories weir here ring"

"Sum won or tabby maid toot ache theory sponsor Billy tea."

"Own lit rub Liz weave scene nit tall biff ore. Though sewer tube lame actor Lynne a scent. Anne Denny weigh, gnome at a watt their a queues dove, the lonely may kegs queue says four reacher there."

"Press icily. Aye cud hunters edit bet a mice elf."

"Two write! Ice head eggs act lea this aim tomb eye why phone Leah fume in knit sag owe."

"There awl tour can know whack shun."

"Know yew sir tall."

"Andy few trite ooh chain Jenny thin gab out thumb, Theo lotto thumb a loan lid in I there par tinny tall."

"Can you Billy fit? There clay Ming two knot of a knee eyed ear watt wee a Ron nab out."

The Deaths Of Abraham Plinn

Young Abraham Plinn was just ninety years old
That morning his body was found stiff and cold.
He'd had buttered toast, as he did every day,
And was stirring his tea when he passed away.

The shock made him die again when the doc said:
"Alas, Mrs Plinn, your dear husband is dead."
To die for a second time, that was a shame,
Though being dead already, he wasn't to blame.

He stumbled and tumbled, then fell down like lead.
And got killed again when he banged his poor head.
He carried on talking throughout the next week
Till told he was probably too dead to speak.

He answered: "I've never been taught how to die,
But be patient with me. I'll give it a try."
He sorted his funeral, wrote out a will
And chose the fine coffin his body would fill.

He stood in the graveyard and wished us goodbye
Then lay in his box with a tear in his eye
And after a couple of prayers had been said
We left him to rest with the rest of the dead.

For more than ten years, we heard nothing at all.
Then yesterday evening we had a phone call.
He'd thought it through carefully and rung us to say:
"Please dig me back up. I've decided to stay."

A Modern Viking

When death lent its pallor
To Vikings of valour
Their souls were despatched to Valhalla.

If I were a Viking
I'd stake my claim striking
Blows boldly while fighting for my king.

But as I've no liking
For longboats or hiking,
I guess I'd become the first Viking

To battle with valour
And get to Valhalla
By blading, skate-boarding and biking.

Dragon At A Party

Sidles in slowly and slyly and seedily
Wanders round wilily, wheedling wheezily
Grinning and greeting all gratingly greasily
Chummily, cheerily chattering cheesily

Leerily, beerily back-biting easily
Simpering simply salaciously sleazily
Pedaling scandal unpleasantly pleasedly
Eavesdropping evilly, eyes popping beadily

Hears his hosts' infant is in bed, diseasedly
Creeps upstairs sneakily, creakily, weaselly
Finds where the poor mite is quarantined queasily
Quiets their darling, his teeth closing tweezerly.

Blood, flesh and bone are all cleared away speedily
Lovingly licked up and guzzled down greedily.
Dragons don't mind their meat sickly or measily…

"Wonderful party!" he tells them all breezily
Slips through the door and leaves, easy-peasily.

Four Relatively Silly Poems

1.

I flew in a rocket to **MA**'s
And some **MOTHER** planets too,
Then **FATHER** into space until
The **SON** was out of view

2.

The landlord of the pub **HUSBAND** me.
He chucked me out of the **DAUGHTER** night
Be **COUSIN** a bit of a drunken rage
Ap-**PARENT**-ly I started a fight.

3.

I remem-**BROTHER** nights like this
With a full moon high in an **UNCLE**-ouded sky.
We were young. Life was a **GRANDAD** venture.
A **NIECE TWIN**-d blew and the air was fresh and dry.

4.

WIFE I been itching and twitching
As if I **DAD** chicken-pox?
Because I've got hundreds of **AUNT**s in my pants
A **NEPHEW** more in my socks.

Dean McBean

who sat too long at his computer

When young Dean McBean
Became over-keen
On his computer
Games machine
Twenty-four-seven
He sat at the screen.

There he stayed stuck
As if he'd been glued
And slept not one wink
Nor ate any food
And, if interrupted,
Just flew in a mood
And then either grunted
Or got very rude.

Now, no-one need put up
With that attitude
And such was the course
His poor parents pursued.
They did their own thing,
As did their young dude.

Well boys, as a breed,
Are not notably clean,
But this lad abandoned
All trace of hygiene.
The smell as he wasted
Away and grew lean
Soon rendered his room
A malodorous scene.

The little now left of him
Literally stank,
A stench which grew stronger
While he himself shrank,
His feet foully fetid,
His hair liced and lank.
His home, by osmosis,
Turned equally rank,
A state into which
The whole neighbourhood sank.

The Council responded
When people complained.
Committees were formed
And convened and maintained.
The stench was examined
But never explained
In countless reports
Using gallons of ink
Each printed in triplicate
(White, blue and pink)
Concluding that no-one
Knew quite what to think.

Young Dean, in the meantime,
Had withered and died.
His folks were relieved,
That can't be denied.
Each stifled a smile
And neither one cried
But bought a cheap coffin
And put him inside.

His fat and flesh gone,
He was just bone and hide
With space for computer
And games by his side.
The lid then got slid on,
And screws were applied
And straight off the odour
Began to subside.

With room, house and
neighbourhood
Freed from the smell,
The Council claimed credit
For lifting the spell.
The local press headline
Read: "Rescued From Hell"
And an ad on page fifteen,
Beneath 'Buy and Sell'
Said: "Need a computer desk?
Give us a bell.
We've got a bedroom
To rent now as well".

So learn from the fate
Of the late Dean McBean
And don't become glued
To your computer screen.

There's A Lot That I've Not Seen

I've seen no sunbathers at night.
I've seen no pens taught how to write.
I've seen no combs with teeth that bite.

I've seen no chair-legs learn to walk.
I've seen no knife that kissed a fork.
I've seen no mouse that caught a hawk.

I've seen no thirty-foot tall elves.
I've seen no books climb on their shelves.
I've seen no meals consume themselves.

I've seen no puddle waterproof.
I've seen no seahorse stamp its hoof.
I've seen no cellar on a roof.

I've seen no tree that won a race.
I've seen no shoe tie its own lace.
I've seen no fish in outer space.

I've seen no sky that's been bright green.
I've seen no jack that beats a queen.
I've seen no twelve that's called twoteen...

I've seen no things that I've not seen.

Loud Music

The walls are all shaking.
The paintwork is flaking.
But why do they blame it on us?
And dad's belly-aching
Cos windows are breaking.
What is it he wants to discuss?
That grandma is waking.
The neighbours are quaking.
Oh, why does he make such a fuss?

We're moshing. We're rocking.
They may say that's shocking.
But why do they blame it on us?
Now neighbours are flocking.
They're shouting. They're knocking.
What is it they want to discuss?
Our door needs unlocking.
Their ears need unblocking.
Oh, why do they make such a fuss?

Mum nags and dad rants on
Like his pants have ants in.
But why do they blame it on us?
And grandma is prancing
And screeching out: "Grandson!"
What is it she wants to discuss?
I mean, we're just dancing
To Marilyn Manson.
Oh, why do they make such a...
      why do they make such a...
      why do they make such a fuss?

Victorian Diarist

My name is Ebenezer Gray.
I wear my top-hat every day,
But take it off to go to bed
And put my nightcap on instead.
Before I sleep, I always write,
In Indian ink by candlelight,
Neat notes nibbed in copperplate
On what I've known and done that date.

It's the diary of Ebenezer Gray
Who wore his top-hat all that day
And, though each day is much the same,
He fills its page, then snuffs the flame.
And downstairs, in the darkened hall,
The tall clock stands, with back to wall.
It ticks and tuts, solemnly dour,
And, all night, chimes to mark the hour.

Undreaming, Ebenezer Gray,
Who'll wear his top-hat all today,
Is roused by maid with morning meal.
Outside, the sounds of hoof and wheel.
Now nearer noises fill his room,
Of shoveled coal and driven broom;
While waking smells of baking bread
Give way to polish, soaps, blacklead.

Good morning, Ebenezer Gray!
Your top-hat's there again today.
You're trimmed and tailored, looking fine,
Stiff collar upright, like your spine.
You've breakfasted on bread and kippers.
You've read The Times in gown and slippers.
Now, groomed and dressed with waxed moustache,
You're dapper, without being flash.

Yes, I am Ebenezer Gray.
I wear this top-hat every day.
I pause to raise it when I meet
An old acquaintance in the street.
We nod and smile to be polite,
Though conversation wouldn't be right.
Besides, I very rarely speak,
Save once or maybe twice a week.

So there goes Ebenezer Gray,
Top-hatted for another day.
Across the park with walking-cane,
He strides to horse-drawn tram or train.
At five fifteen, he's home again,
His life a pattern he'll maintain
Till death comes knocking on his door
In the Spring of 1894.

Slow Service At The Tortoise Garage

In the German township of Kassel
Just two blocks down from The Dragon Hotel
On the forecourt of the tortoise Shell
Petrol station, Mademoiselle
The Countess Lady Isabel,
Dragoness de Neufchatel,
Has been waiting quite a lengthy spell
In her pink Volkswagen Caravelle.

She sips a glass of muscatel,
Having told her toad chauffeur, Marcel,
That she thought he ought to jolly well
Get out and ring that service bell
And tell the slowcoach personnel
To hurry up and – what-the-hell –
Raise his voice and really yell
The French word "Vite!", the German "Schnell!"

This, she's sure, should now propel
These tortoises to serve and sell
Some petrol for her Caravelle.
It's a faith which time will soon dispel
For tortoises, unlike gazelle,
So gradually shift, you can hardly tell.
More slothful than sloths, they're without parallel,
Their slowness the one thing at which they excel.

If you're in a hurry, avoid Kassel,
The city in which the tortoises dwell.
Why, it'll be hours before Mademoiselle
The Countess Lady Isabel,
Dragoness de Neufchatel,
And her put-upon chauffeur, poor Marcel,
Can bid the flat forecourt farewell
And drive off past The Dragon Hotel.

The Demolition Giant

Dark stone released
This brick-built beast
Manmade, mostly,
Partly ghostly,
Ghastly, towering,
Overpowering;
A body based
On building waste
With every trace of flesh replaced.

He's firstly, lastly,
Ever so vastly
Made out of debris.
He's rubbly, pebbly,
Doubly, trebly
Bigger than you and me.

Got bricks and dirt
Inside his shirt,
Great big boulders
For his shoulders,
Sides of houses
In his trousers,
A sturdy belt
Of grey asphalt
And a coat of old carpet and under-felt.

He's rumbly, grumbly,
Terribly crumbly,
Humbly tumbledown too.
He's rubbly, pebbly,
Doubly, trebly
Bigger than me and you.

In place of bones
Are paving stones,
And all his veins
Are pipes and drains
In which the blood's
A flood of mud,
While x-ray charts
Reveal his heart's
Old central heating boiler parts.

He differs from us.
He's broad as a bus,
Taller than a tree.
He's rubbly, pebbly,
Doubly, trebly
Bigger than you and me.

He's got a stride
Ten metres wide,
With concrete blocks
Inside his socks.
His roof-beam arms
Have doorstep palms,
While bags of sand,
I understand,
Form the fingers of each hand.

He's mumbly, bumbly,
Somewhat stumbly,
One of the fumbly few.
He's rubbly, pebbly,
Doubly, trebly
Bigger than me and you.

His fireplace gob's
A cobbled job;
The teeth, in clumps
Of crooked stumps,
Are broken plates
And tiles and slates
He grinds and grates
As he contemplates...
Nothing at all... just stands outside and waits.

He's mouldy and old
And feels the cold.
We hardly reach his knee.
He's rubbly, pebbly,
Doubly, trebly
Bigger than you and me.

His hair's odd things
Like ropes and strings
And old bed-springs,
Long chains of ring
And wiry things.
It curls and clings,
Then suddenly swings
And lifts, like wings,
And sparkles like the wealth of kings.

He's crusty, dusty,
Dreadfully musty;
Justifiably blue.
He's rubbly, pebbly,
Doubly, trebly
Bigger than me and you.

His face ain't quaint,
It's peeling paint
With a brash moustache
That's bits of trash.
His dim eyesight's
Frosted skylights.
And when he blows
That chimney nose,
A sort of sooty slime fills his hankie, I suppose.

Cos firstly, lastly,
Ever so vastly
He's made of debris.
He's rubbly, pebbly,
Doubly, trebly
Bigger than you and me.

Recycling Michael

We're gonna recycle
My mate Michael...

Give his goofy teeth
To toothless Keith,
Have his gormless grin
As a rubbish bin.
But who wants skin with spots and zits
Or clumps of hair with knots and nits?

We're gonna recycle
My mate Michael...

Use his shouts and screams and moans,
To fill foghorns and megaphones.
Re-builders want his clomping feet
To kick down walls and smash concrete.
But what'll we do with his lazy brains
And his blazer covered in gravy stains?

We're gonna recycle
My mate Michael...

Lend the rumbles in his tum
To an orchestra as a big bass drum,
Sell his bogies, burps and farts
To galleries as works of art.
But how on Earth do we dispose
Of those lugholes and that huge nose?

We're gonna recycle
My mate Michael...

Make good use of his knobbly knees
For filing nails and grating cheese.
His nipping, slapping, punching hands
Can wage our wars in foreign lands.
But who'll have all his moody rants
Or save the world from his underpants?

Other Children's Books By Nick Toczek

Number, Number, Cut A Cucumber (Caboodle '09)

Cats'n'Bats'n'Slugs'n'Bugs (Caboodle '08)

Read Me Out Loud! (Macmillan '07)

Dragons! The Musical (Golden Apple '05)

Dragons! (Macmillan '05)

The Dog Ate My Bus Pass (Macmillan '04)

Sleeping Beauty's Dream (Golden Apple '03)

Kick It! (Macmillan '02)

Number Parade (LDA '02)

Can Anyone Be As Gloomy As Me? (Hodder '00,
    republished '05)

Toothpaste Trouble (Macmillan '02)

The Dragon Who Ate Our School (Macmillan '00)

Never Stare at a Grizzly Bear (Macmillan '00)

Join In... Or Else! (Macmillan '00)

Dragons Everywhere (Macmillan '97)

Dragons (Macmillan '95)